studio art

studio art
a resource for artist-teachers

Larry T. Schultz

VAN NOSTRAND REINHOLD COMPANY
New York Cincinnati Toronto London Melbourne

To the outstanding art teachers of the Jefferson County Schools and two master art consultants, Frank Tresise and Lester Burbank Bridaham. My special thanks to Jan

Van Nostrand Reinhold Company Regional Offices:
New York   Cincinnati   Chicago   Millbrae   Dallas
Van Nostrand Reinhold Company International Offices:
London   Toronto   Melbourne

Library of Congress Catalog Card Number 75-155588
ISBN 0-442-27433-5
ISBN 0-442-27433-0 (paper)

Manufactured in Singapore

Published in 1973 by Van Nostrand Reinhold Company
A Division of Litton Educational Publishing, Inc.
450 West 33rd Street, New York, N.Y. 10001
Published simultaneously in Canada by
Van Nostrand Reinhold Ltd.
16 15 14 13 12 11 10 9 8 7 6 5 4 3 2 1

The author and Van Nostrand Reinhold Company
have taken all possible care to trace the ownership
of every work of art reproduced in this book and to
make full acknowledgment for its use. If any errors
have accidentally occurred, they will be corrected in
subsequent editions, provided notification is sent to
the publisher.

contents

introduction

The studio-art program contains sequential, content-oriented units of drawing, painting, printmaking, and three-dimensional design. In Lost in the Forest, a woodcut from the printmaking unit by Marcia Ott (age 13), a background of trees heightens emotion in the man's face

Those who are or would be art teachers have a responsibility for education that transcends the art room and the students who learn there. They must help educate parents, teachers, community, and the school administrators who fund programs and decide priorities. If art education is to realize its potential and promise, its advocates must find a way to introduce it into more school programs. Less than half of the nation's junior and senior high schools offer art as an elective subject! For many public-school students at the elementary and secondary level, art has been merely a seasonal experience of chalk turkeys or cut-and-colored-paper Christmas trees. For many administrators art has been a tolerated frill, barely supported by funds, or a necessary scheduling device to handle increasing enrollments.

Art educators must learn what makes an art program effective, and then they must specify strategies to ensure the adoption of an art education curriculum that will provide students with an exciting and rewarding learning experience. For the better part of the past decade I have been working toward that goal as an art coordinator in a 75,000-pupil school district in Jefferson County, Colorado. The requirements, as I see it, for making an art education program good enough to be on a par with other school programs are as follows:

1. A well-defined, sequential curriculum
2. Art materials enough to fit a diversity of talent, enrollment, and space
3. Adequate time for instruction, teacher self-improvement, and development of each pupil's creativity
4. Sufficient space for a student-centered program capable of growing with increased demand
5. Support for curriculum development and innovation
6. Informed administrators
7. Well-qualified, enthusiastic instructors

This book details one art program, studio art, that is a strategy for combining the seven basic requirements listed above. It evolved from discussions with art educators and school administrators. First of all, the teachers specified an "ideal" program designed to provide the best learning experiences. Together, we studied existing programs, and from their best elements constructed a flexible, sequential curriculum that approached our ideal. It included units of drawing, painting, printmaking, and three-dimensional design to be studied in roughly nine-week sections, as well as art history and other elements incorporated throughout. After identifying materials, equipment, and space needed, we implemented a series of pilot programs consisting of instructional units that varied from six weeks at the elementary level to a full year in secondary schools.

This pilot program was further refined by school administrators, who were receptive because of its clearly defined needs and objectives. Administrators not only supported it with funds, space, and enthusiasm, but they helped to introduce the approach to their art teachers, and asked them to analyze facilities, programs, and techniques to see what part of the studio-art approach they could adopt. Alternative times were allocated for art classes in the existing school scheduling, especially at the elementary level where more instruction time was needed. Release time was obtained for teachers who wanted to enrich their own teaching by working with consultants.

Studio art is simply an approach that breaks basic art-instruction units such as drawing, painting, etc. into sequential skills. The student learns the basic skills first, and then through experimentation, exploration, and creative design progresses to skills with new and varied approaches. He builds on what he has learned in the past and what he hopes to gain in the future.

As the name of the program implies, the art room is very important in the studio-art approach. No matter what kind of room or space is available, the art teacher organizes it specifically to serve the needs of the program. The four basic units — drawing, painting, printmaking, and three-dimensional design — each have their own equipment, work-space, and storage requirements. In addition, blackout facilities, special lighting for critiques and a student resource center — for viewing slides and using reference books — should be built into the physical plan from the start.

In the past, art teachers were expected to accept the room they were given and then to tailor the program to the room's limitations. In the studio-art approach, the program dictates the redesigning of the room. Whether the room is large or small, limited or adequate, students benefit by working in an area that looks like a studio rather than an ordinary, closed classroom. Teachers are encouraged to plan for these facilities with school administrators who are responsible for equipment and the physical plant.

It is difficult to measure results in the business of teaching art, but some yardsticks are necessary to determine the value of each new approach. The only measure I have found valuable is growth. The program's growth can be measured by the number of students taking art as an elective, the students' growth can be roughly estimated by honors and awards they win. The reputation of a program grows, too. This can be measured by increased administrative support, recognition by the community (and its professional artists), and most important, by the teachers' acceptance.

The change in teachers is the most startling phenomenon I have observed as a result of the studio-art program. Time and again I have seen the rebirth of professional commitment and personal vitality. Because teachers accepted the responsibility for teaching in a new way, they came alive while experimenting with new media, programs, and ideas. As they continually developed their own artistic skills in this way, their talent became infectious — and their students caught the excitement.

In a very real sense, a new breed of instructor emerged: the artist-teacher. By inviting students to visit artists' studios and exhibits in the community and by inviting artists to the classroom to assist and demonstrate, the instructor became a living resource for art. The artist-teacher uses his participation in the cultural resources of the community — college courses, art seminars, and exhibits — to alert the students to the arts. By welcoming innovation, the artist-teacher serves as an agent for change.

A teacher or school system contemplating changes like these will be justifiably cautious because of past difficulties in getting the necessary time, space, equipment, and administrative support. However, many schools are moving toward the studio approach. The program has attracted the support of the Charles F. Kettering Foundation, the J.D.R. 3rd Fund, Central Midwestern Regional Educational Laboratory, Inc. (CEMREL), and the National Endowment for the Arts. Administrative support for individual programs has doubled since the change to studio art. Where a traditional art room's equipment inventory amounted to less than $300, some principals have willingly spent $3,000 to $5,000 in initiating a studio-art program.

Although it is difficult to measure, enthusiasm has been shown in many other ways for the program. *Scholastic Voice* and *Junior Scholastic* magazines selected artwork from our junior- and senior-high art programs for their May 1971 covers. Artists in the community have been willing to share their experiences in workshops, seminars, and tours through their studios. The real test of the program — student appeal — has been passed with flying colors. Where the art program is completely elective on the junior- and senior-high level, it has been necessary to double the number of instructors. Reports from some principals indicate that the growth in enrollment would be even larger if there were facilities enough to handle it.

The following chapters focus principally on student work. Most of the illustrations come from the junior-high level, where the studio-art program began. Because of its success at the junior-high level the studio-art approach easily spread to elementary and senior-high levels. Any of the sequential steps and recommended resources can be used at all these levels as long as the teacher adapts them to the particular needs of the class.

Student work is not only the product of individual talents, but also of arduous effort by teachers. In the studio-art program, their challenge involves more than personal gain for themselves and their classes. It is a commitment to a cooperative effort, a pooling of resources, that can have far-reaching benefits. It can work in your school, school district, or state. We know that it works for us, and we are not unique.

Crayon still life, from the drawing unit, by Jim Hoskinson (age 14)

Girl With Lillies, acrylic on white detail drawing paper, from the painting unit, by Dwight Cocovinis (age 14)

The studio-art approach fosters a new breed of instructor, the artist-teacher, who demonstrates his own talents and skills for his class

Ninth grade hand-built ceramic pots and batiks with strong emphasis on surface design, from the three-dimensional design unit. (Photo by Unity)

Students build skills by developing what they
have learned in previous units. This white
tempera drawing on black construction paper
by Debbie Richardson (age 13) shows a
mastery of surface design that will be easily
carried over to printmaking

Woman, Window, Pill, transfer drawing by Ina
Gustafsen (age 15). Turpentine is applied to
material from newspapers and magazines,
and then the image is rubbed off onto the
surface of the paper. Compositions obtained
in this way can be reworked in any suitable
medium

designing a studio

A studio is not just an art room but a space that has the look and feel of an artist's work area. Here, students have successfully redecorated a *WWII* barracks into an imaginative environment for learning

A good studio-art program requires an art room that does not perpetuate the dull sameness of most of this nation's schools. I have visited art rooms that had the same ceramic tile, the same school-district-green walls, and the same washed-out brown window shades as the rest of the building. Art educators, who are expected to teach visual awareness, cannot do it properly in such a visually boring environment. Instead, they should begin their planning by remembering the studio that most made them want to work and study in it, and then try to re-create it in the classroom. Above and beyond the equipment and art supplies in an art room, its atmosphere can have a direct and stimulating effect on students.

A studio, then, is not just an art room in the traditional sense, but a space that has the look and feel of an artist's studio and is tailored to the needs of the particular program the teacher is conducting within its confines. The studio must be a comfortable, functional place to work, and must reflect the individuality of the artist-teacher, who will spend one year at least, and probably many more in the studio.

We must overcome the idea that schools are operated for maintenance men and custodians, and begin to realize that they are for the particular needs of students and teachers. And the needs of art teachers and students are essentially different from those of academic classes. Nevertheless, most art rooms are barely changed versions of the standard, closed schoolroom, perhaps because architects and administrators seem to have a preconceived concept of what an art room should be: a tidy, all-purpose area in which most of what is being taught is a mystery to them. The art teacher or administrator who helps to change this idea will not only be providing a more creative space — one that is different in texture and color from any other place in the school — but he will be making a more functional art area as well.

When six professional artists were invited by a combined program of the National Endowment for the Arts and CEMREL to conduct school programs during the 1969-70 academic year, five of them found that the assigned, traditional art room was most unsuitable for conducting their activities. One of the artists completely repainted and remodeled the area before he moved in because he couldn't stand working in a "classroom green" room.

The problems in planning new studios or remodeling old ones are the same — inadequate space, lack of storage facilities, scanty equipment. Each teacher will find new ways of coping with them, and the solutions will differ as well as the costs. The following suggestions for designing a studio actually have been put into effect in eighteen schools.

None had the same budget for equipment or remodeling and all differed in final costs, from less than $1000 to as much as $8000 for remodeling and outfitting. However, funds were programed for these purposes, even if the changes had to be spread out over a period of two or three years. In some cases, the principal has become so interested that he has initiated much of the change, and has become actively involved in seeing that his teachers are well provided for. Naturally, the cost estimates will vary from area to area and from year to year, but some idea of what the studio-art program encountered in the last decade may provide a useful jumping-off point for the future.

Designing a studio is essentially two different problems: initial planning in a new building and remodeling or adapting to existing facilities. In either case, it is important for the individual art teacher to make the essential decisions about his teaching space because he is going to spend a great part of his life there. Consequently, he knows better than anyone how it should be planned. The suggestions in this chapter are broad and general, but the teacher must be specific.

For the artist-teacher who is lucky enough to be in a district where a new building is being planned, the problem is one of taking a completely new look at available facilities and equipment from the point of view of the artist's studio, and then planning accordingly. Also he must specifically communicate his special needs to designers and draftsmen — storage for over-sized projects, work areas for "messy" activities, space for special groupings such as class drawing from a model, and other things that only an art teacher is alert to. Art departments have rarely planned this way (although home economics, technical arts, and science departments have done so for years), and consequently funds and designs for art needs are not generally well developed. The art teacher who is given an opportunity to plan comprehensively in advance must present his ideas in a practical fashion and in order of priority of his needs, especially where budgets are tight.

For the great number of teachers using already existing art rooms, the problem of implementing a studio-art program revolves around adapting to an already inadequate design. All the ingenuity a teacher is capable of will be needed in conserving space, sharing ideas and supplies with other teachers, and applying a lot of elbow grease — the teacher often has to do the remodeling himself, if it is to be done at all. Frequently it is easier to relocate the art room than to remodel it, and many times a larger space is available right in the building. As long as the studio is thought of as a place of work, not a shiny showcase, supplies are fairly easy to come by. For example, teachers of other subjects may be discarding furniture that can serve an art class very well. Sometimes students who are actively involved in the design or remodeling work can come up with excellent, unusual solutions.

Space is a prime requirement in all rooms, whether old or new. One studio for every 350 students enrolled is a workable ratio, and a school of 1000 students should never have less than two studios, ideally three. Total school capacity should be projected in planning for studio space because growth in enrollment will affect the art program as well as the rest of the school.

An art room should never be smaller than 1500 square feet, and the storage area should be an additional 300 square feet at least. The artwork in this book was done in rooms that varied between 800 and 1600 square feet; needless to say, the teachers with larger spaces to work in had more flexibility and greater opportunities to develop creative programs. (It is always wise to ask for more than enough space, and then settle later for the adequate figure.)

The average art room requires approximately $6,500 in special equipment — kilns, potter's wheels, printing presses, hand tools, ceramic equipment, projectors, brushes, paper cutters, etc. This estimate does not include the necessary tables, workbenches, and other fixed furniture and "hardware" such as lighting and cabinets, all of which generally amounts to another $6,500. In addition, a studio must be well supplied with "software" — paper, books, filmstrips, slides, paints, brushes, clay — some of which can be collected in a resource center. This open, or closed, area is a basic library of books, slides, prints, and audio-visual equipment that should be in a separate but student-accessible area of the studio.

The art room should have a multitude of locked storage cabinets, north light, and if possible an exit to an outside patio for clay, sculpture, and sketching. A studio should never have fewer than two sinks, both double and deep, and supplied with drain traps for clay. Preferably, they should be located at opposite ends of the room to avoid traffic jams and other complications. There should be blackout shades, a permanent screen for showing slides and filmstrips, electrical outlets for both 110 and 220 volts, and adjustable studio lights that can be projected on student work, still-life arrangements, prints, and other materials that should be lighted properly for display and critiques.

In initial planning, some of the important requirements such as adequate space, proper natural lighting, location near plumbing, and good storage areas can be specified from the very beginning, and thus the usual inadequacies of traditional art rooms can be avoided. What would a studio look like if the artist-teacher had all the freedom in the world to design for his needs? In addition to providing for special preferences, the teacher should follow most of the space and cost guidelines given above, where possible. In schools that have more than one art teacher, the art rooms can be designed individually — one for the special needs of drawing, painting, and print-making and the others for three-dimensional design such as sculpture and ceramics.

After deciding what type of storage is most fitting for the classes' needs — with locks or without, with doors or open, containing fixed or adjustable shelving — the teacher should draw a plan for a storage area that will accommodate all of the paper and materials he plans to use. The people who design cabinetwork for schools may not know that art paper comes in several sizes, from 9 x 12 inches to 36 x 24 inches and larger. Nor do they seem to realize that the standard individual storage areas — small plastic trays that require all work to be rolled if larger than 9 x 12 inches — are quite inefficient for art students. Instead, a flat, adjustable set of shelves, in a bin at least 24 x 36 inches, should be designed for storing student drawings and paintings. There are some standard blueprint cabinets on the market that may also serve the purpose of flat storage.

Interest in independent work can be stimulated if a student has the chance to search through a resource center for materials related to his project. Space for this area should be set aside in the plans, and lighting built in to accompany it for group presentations. As a particular unit is being presented, many teachers like to dim the lights in the room and show slides on the topic. (It is a very simple matter to install rheostat control, so that the lights can be dimmed or brightened with a simple adjustment, when lighting fixtures are first connected in a room.) Films, books, and prints for the resource center can be obtained from many sources, including the National Art Education Association and the local state department of education. The necessary addresses are probably in the teacher's own school library — and the librarian usually will volunteer to do the ordering. Further information can be obtained from book publishers, who are usually happy to send catalogs on request, and from educational film companies. Many films and slides are available for rental, and if only one showing is necessary, some companies will send films and slides for free preview.

To ensure that his plans will be communicated undistorted, the teacher should take the initiative in working directly with those responsible for the planning of the studio. As long as he has his points clearly in mind, he should be able to communicate his specifications to most architects and designers.

Remodeling or Relocating

The artist-teacher faced with implementing a studio-art program in an already planned and equipped art room has a more difficult problem than one who has been able to plan his own room. He must first take stock of all the space available in the room — sometimes traditional necessities such as the teacher's desk can be eliminated or moved. In one instance a principal agreed to let an art class switch to a larger room that had been wasted on a mathematics class. The math class adjusted itself easily to the 800 square-foot room that originally had been assigned to an art class.

After the space inventory, the teacher should take stock of his furniture, electrical capacity, and plumbing facilities to determine what is still needed. The standard tables, chairs, and cupboards can sometimes be supplemented by supplies in the school — benches that technical arts departments have discarded may be well suited for the rough work necessary to clay and sculpture units. Cabinets that have been returned to the school-maintenance department because of scratches or broken doors can be utilized in any studio. The broken doors can be removed altogether if the special storage needs of the class require open shelves.

Furniture can be constructed as well as being obtained ready-made. Drawing benches or horses can be constructed with plywood in the technical arts department, or a local carpenter can make them at minimum cost. Drawing boards, 26 x 36 inches, can be made very inexpensively from ⅛-inch tempered Masonite. Storage units can be constructed economically from pine or Masonite if expensive features such as doors and locks are not required.

There is not much that a teacher can do to supplement scanty sink and wet-area facilities, but he can install additional lighting. Most electrical shops in cities and towns of any size have catalogs picturing display lights that are simple to connect and cost less than $150. If limited funds make such a purchase impossible, a simple extension cord looped over a hook will serve as a wiring connection between a fixture in the ceiling and some sort of spotlight.

Most schools plan remodeling budgets six months or a year in advance, so the studio-art teacher must have his ideas down in black and white, in order of priority. Materials on hand should be utilized to the fullest — especially in supplies that will not be depleted, such as audio-visual equipment and books and prints for the resource center — and with each successive budget, the collection can be enlarged.

Relocating the art class may be easier than adapting to an inadequate art room. The most common change that has occurred in the studio-art programs has been relocation coupled with remodeling, often producing a dramatic change in appearance. Many of the schools in the program have access to old buildings, and, as a result, studio work is carried on in a congenial atmosphere of paneled walls, weathered wood, and shake shingles. One teacher requested the use of a farm barn near the school. The teacher and students have painted, collected interesting objects for decoration, and displayed wall hangings to brighten their studios.

There are many opportunities waiting for city art teachers, too. The Parkway project in Philadelphia is an example of a school-without-walls approach in which non-school buildings have been made available to students. At the University of Michigan, the entire ceramics program moved into a vacant automobile dealer's establishment. In St. Louis, an artist-teacher relocated the studio-art program into a large, empty storage building. Proposals like these raise a multitude of insurance and liability questions and state and industrial code standards. But unless the art educator gives his plan a try, no one will ever know whether or not it can become a reality.

As bond issues continue to fail, and classes are more and more overcrowded, teachers and administrators must take advantage of other spaces for classroom facilities. In the existing studio-art programs several schools have utilized neglected library areas while moving the library into other open space in the building. Four art departments have moved into temporary buildings outside the main school building; nine departments have cut openings into adjoining rooms in order to expand. One teacher has convinced the school counselor that his office, now adjoining the art room, should become the three-dimensional area, while his desk can be moved into another nearby space. In Philadelphia an abandoned lunchroom was pressed into use, in San Diego, it was a large special-education room with a skylight, and in Jefferson County, an auto-mechanics building was converted. In St. Paul a basement was remodeled for a sculpture studio.

No matter how small, any remodeling or relocation effort serves a purpose as an example to other administrators and educators. As new schools are constructed, those requests for space and facilities that are based solidly on past experience will have a better chance of being granted. The studio-art program in our 9 high schools has grown from less than 10 per cent of total school enrollment (10 per cent is the average high-school art enrollment throughout the United States) to well over 20 per cent. From such figures, future school boards and administrators can conclude that curriculum changes, supported by changes in the physical plan of the studio, have made art more attractive to students.

The needs of art teachers and students are essentially different from those of academic classes

Large equipment demands a redesigning of available space. Printing presses, however, are luxuries because fine prints can be made with a spoon, as were the majority of the prints in this book

Adapting existing storage facilities is one of the most difficult problems. A brush rack made from wood scraps and clothespins is one handy solution

A clothesline stretched across the studio for hanging drying prints is convenient in-progress storage. (Photo by Unity)

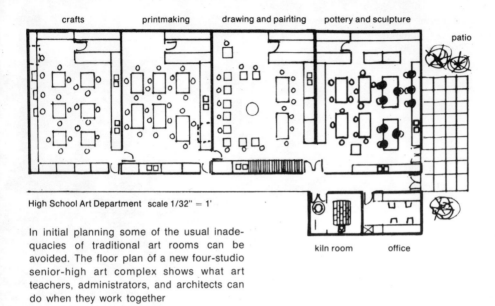

crafts   printmaking   drawing and painting   pottery and sculpture

patio

High School Art Department scale 1/32" = 1'

kiln room   office

In initial planning some of the usual inadequacies of traditional art rooms can be avoided. The floor plan of a new four-studio senior-high art complex shows what art teachers, administrators, and architects can do when they work together

The crafts studio in the art complex includes various sizes of cabinets and convenient storage for tools. (Photo by Phillips)

The printmaking studio provides for high, overhead storage and adjustable shelving. (Photo by Phillips)

The drawing and painting studio allows great flexibility in work arrangements and ample vertical storage. (Photo by Phillips)

The teacher planning office. (Photo by Phillips)

The pottery and sculpture studio is arranged so students can circulate freely while carrying on a variety of activities. The wet areas are conveniently located on back wall. (Photo by Phillips)

The kiln room. (Photo by Phillips)

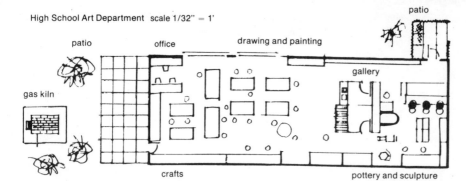

High School Art Department scale 1/32" = 1'

patio

patio

office

drawing and painting

gallery

gas kiln

crafts

pottery and sculpture

As classes become more and more over-crowded, teachers and administrators must take advantage of other space. This plan shows a functional and attractive art studio developed from the existing structure of an old auto-mechanics shop. The minor remodelling changes were done completely by teacher and students

The exterior of the remodelled auto-mechanics shop. Entrance to the studio is shown in the foreground. (Photo by Phillips)

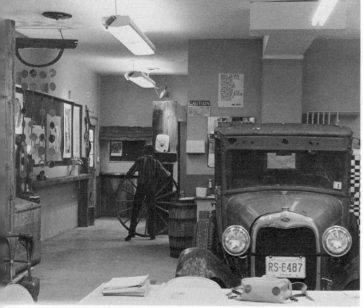

The largest area of this open classroom is for drawing and painting — still lifes as big as a car can be moved in and out easily! (Photo by Phillips)

The drawing area, teacher's planning area (shown at right rear) and storage. All of the furniture had been discarded by science and cafeteria rooms. (Photo by Phillips)

The gallery area was remodelled to have its own entrance from the patio. (Photo by Phillips)

The pottery and sculpture area (gallery in background) was completely constructed by the art teacher and students out of used materials, including a now-decorated old bathtub for clay (Photo by Phillips)

The pottery and sculpture area is divided from the gallery by a very serviceable showcase constructed out of rough lumber. (Photo by Phillips)

studio drawing

A drawing unit should be organized with tables or drawing benches and a stand for still lifes or a platform for a model that is elevated enough to give all the students a good view

The most basic unit in the studio-art approach is drawing; from drawing skills the student can enrich his techniques in an orderly way as he progresses through painting and printmaking to three-dimensional design. The unit on drawing, like the others, is presented in a series of skill exercises of roughly nine weeks from which the student can explore and create new techniques.

Every art educator has a method of teaching drawing that he feels comfortable with, and he should use it. The important point about implementing a studio-art program is not to define rigid categories of exercises from which neither the teacher or the student derive any creative enthusiasm, but to develop an outline hand-tailored to the artist-teacher and his class, one that is flexible enough to allow experimentation and enrichment from other sources while at the same time providing a basic repertoire of skills. This book contains work from many schools and many individual studio-art programs, and the strategies it offers have been collected from many exciting teachers.

The physical setup of the studio in the drawing unit is most important because so many model-drawing and still-life exercises are done. From the outset, the teacher should arrange the studio to facilitate group drawing — tables and drawing benches arranged around a stand for still lifes or a platform for a model that is elevated enough to give all students a good view. The stand should be placed where the lighting is best, or where it can be changed easily when shadowing effects are to be stressed. Far too many teachers place an orange and a wine bottle at one end of the room, at desk level, without considering what a student's view would be from each position in the room.

Drawing often presents the worst problems in getting proper furniture for work and storage — there is nothing worse than trying to draw on a piece of paper that is larger than the board! On the other hand, its special requirements can set a tone for the studio class that can carry through the whole course. For example, merely rearranging the chairs and benches will awaken students, who generally sit in rows in academic classes, to the fact that an art class is something special. It is a good idea for young people to stand for the beginning figure studies at least, and the removal of chairs can help remove some of the old notions of what art education is like. Every student should have a small box of art tools and materials, most of which can be found around the house. Giving students a list of tools they will need — brushes, pencils, charcoal, sticks, and pens — shows them that the art class is not a place to spend time with a borrowed pencil and nothing else.

There are several types of drawing, from freehand to mechanical perspective and computer art. Showing contemporary examples and master freehand drawings from the resource center gives students a glimpse of the range and variety inherent in drawn line. Excellent examples of drawn illustrations can be found in magazines such as *Fortune* and *Sports Illustrated.*

A unit of introductory exercises should last about four or five days. The students should begin with simple contour drawings of models chosen from the class. (The students will be more interested in solving this drawing problem if they have chosen the model and, in later exercises, what he or she will wear.) The beginning contour drawings should be three to five minutes, which allows several to be done in every class. A time limit on each drawing prevents the student from laboring over what should be a quick and fresh impression. Felt-tip pen, which flows over paper easily, encourages the idea of a quick, flowing drawing, and newsprint as a drawing support reinforces the idea of a temporary exercise. While drawing blind contours, the students should not be constrained by shading and shadow; art students can be kept free in their movements if occasionally they draw with the other hand from the one they use for writing.

Following four or five days of drawing simply from male and female models, the students are ready to begin working on the qualities of line, tone, and color. A drawing at this stage should not last longer than one class period, because the students do not enjoy carrying problems over two or three classes until they are more skilled. A drawing pencil can be introduced — 4B is a good choice — and the work done on construction paper of some light color. Crayon highlights can be used to complete the pose. Because costuming is so exciting to young people, it is a good idea to introduce it slowly; a football uniform borrowed from the gym department is a familiar but interesting contour for these second-stage drawings.

Once the students are accustomed to models posing in street clothes and familiar gear, they more readily accept unusual attire. Modeled, shaded, or washed drawings can be introduced when working from a figure in leotards, which closely conforms to the body's shape, and the students will begin to feel comfortable with the terminology used in anatomy. A 6B pencil is a good choice as a basic tool, but the tools should be varied — felt-tip pen, pen and ink, a stick for drawing. Students should become accustomed to handling different sizes of paper, too.

Completed drawings should not be the aim. Rather, the need for expressive line should be communicated, perhaps by stopping the class before any drawings are fully finished to show good examples of expressive line. If the studio has been set up conveniently for critiques, the teacher can darken the room, turn on the studio lights, and discuss good and bad examples. It is a real benefit to the students to master a vocabulary for expressing critical terms such as *bold, graceful, interpretive, visually exciting.* The sensitivity to technique, demonstrated by a student who can label a line as *flowing, modeled, gestured, contrasting,* or *curved,* aids in later exploration of new media and new dimensions for expression.

Depending on class and individual student interest, several directions in the studio drawing unit can be taken. A particularly successful one is the completion in three or four class periods of a large, detailed still-life drawing. In the interest of variation and teaching the students to be alert to the visual possibilities of their surroundings, the class can go on a scavenger hunt to build the still life. They might search attics, bring in stuffed or live animals, borrow machinery. Sketching exercises can be found outside the classroom by drawing the scene from the classroom window or going on field trips. A motorcycle or an old car can easily be driven to the school grounds for out-of-doors sketching. Sketches may be finished in the studio in later sessions, or used for practice in capturing fleeting moods of light and color.

The emphasis in these large projects is on light and dark areas, and on the variety that can be achieved through mixing subject matter, various media, and various line techniques. A student who plays the guitar can be both model and still life, while setting the tone of the class with his music. Throughout such explorations the students learn to draw what they see, not what they think they see. And for such a lesson there is no substitute for drawing from nature and from life.

If imagination and interest run thin, which they are not likely to do, the following list may help in the search for sketchbook subjects.

airport
alley
animal
art class
attic
band members
barbershop
basket
basement
beach scene
bicycle
bridge
building site
bus depot
cafe, inside and out
church
city hall
closet
coffeepot
construction men
courthouse
dairy
dishes
dock
downtown area
drugstore

farm
feed mill
festival
filling station
fish, fishing gear
fire escape
fire station
front porch
garage, inside
garden
glass jars
greenhouse
graveyard
hippie
intersection
insect
junk shop
laundry on line
library
locker
lumberyard
machine
motorcycle
museum
musicians, instruments
narrow street

old things: barn, car,
    truck, house, hotel,
    shoes, people
picnic
porch
potted plant
railroad yard
rodeo
rowboat
sailboat
sports, gear and games
sportscar
stairway
teacher
telephone poles
toaster
tools
trash cans
typewriter
utility room
water tower
workshop
yarn
xerox or duplicating machine
zoo

This suggested unit covers several weeks and a variety of media and projects, with time left to take advantage of the resources of the community. Guest artists can provide exciting demonstrations and lectures, or films and slides of artists in their studios can be used to enrich the class's drawing experience. Field trips for sketching might include a stop at a current museum show.

Too many student artists leave an art classroom without evaluating their work or even understanding the problem they were given to solve. It is only by working with the students, by critiquing, criticizing, and complimenting their work, that the teacher can help them grow in the understanding of what they are doing. Yet, part of the gain in visual awareness should be the *teacher's* for he is the greatest single influence on the students. What the class experiences and produces is a direct reflection of his teaching.

Newsprint with tissue paper and felt-tip pen, Kristi Fiske (age 12)

Two Women, bamboo stick, brush, and ink, Connie Baker (age 13)

Pencil (6B) rubbing with emphasis on horizontal line, Nancy Maines (age 14)

Ink drawing, Greg Cross, (age 14). The large letters support the composition in an unusual way

In quick contour drawings students should not be constrained by shading and shadow. Contour drawing, felt-tip pen, Debbie Roberts (age 12)

Contour drawing, felt-tip pen, Tim Sheil (age 13)

Wash techniques are good preparation for shading and for later watercolor paintings. Contour and wash, felt-tip pen, Janice Miller, (age 13)

Pencil (4B) drawing on newsprint, Chris Bogard (age 14)

Because costuming is so exciting to young people it is a good idea to introduce it slowly. Twenty-minute pencil sketch (2B pencil) Steve Carr (age 12)

Pencil drawing on construction paper, shaded with crayon, Arlene Timmons (age 14)

The Red Baron, pencil (2B) drawing on manila paper, Gregg Seastone (age 14)

Students are usually interested in solving a drawing problem if they have chosen the models and their costumes

Pencil (4B) drawing, Scott Brown (age 12)

Ink line and wash of the same model, Mary Mc Donald (age 14)

Girl with Russian Hat, ink line and wash, Robin Cantu (age 14)

Tissue-paper collage and ink, Becky Gardner (age 13)

Ink line and wash of the same model, Sandy Catrine (age 14)

The school counselor was borrowed for an
afternoon

Contour drawing, oil pastel and turpentine,
Gregg Seastone (age 13)

A large detailed still-life drawing can be completed in three or four class periods. The still-life materials were collected by the class on a scavenger hunt

Pencil (2B) drawing of the still life, Mark Carr (age 13)

Pencil (2B) and felt-tip pen drawing, Dwight Cocovinis (age 14)

Tissue paper collage using compositional elements of figures and flowers, Iris Hill (age 14)

Tissue paper collage with abstract design, Diane Wyatt, (age 14). Continuous line was added to give the effect of a transparent design

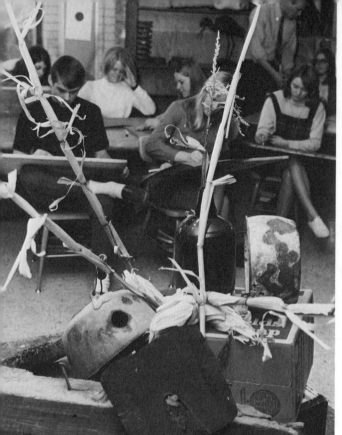

Still life problem requiring students to arrange
their own compositions

Pencil (2B) drawing, Gary Spears (age 14)

Pencil (2B) drawing, Tom Mathews (age 13)

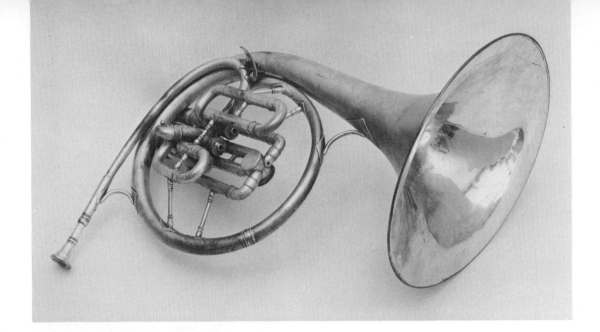

In sketching from objects such as this French horn students learn to achieve variety in mixing subject matter, various media, and various line techniques

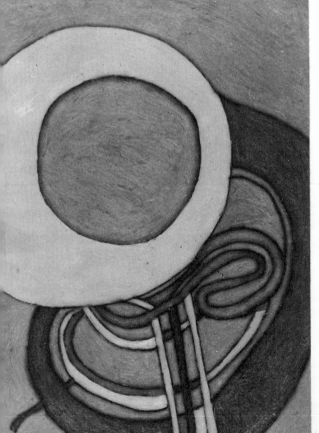

Oil pastel of French horn, Janet DeVigil (age 13). Pastels were pressed evenly and then smoothed

Oil pastel of French horn, Chuck Easton (age 13)

Oil pastel, abstract from French horn, Paul Campbell (age 14)

Oil pastel of violin and case, developing positive and negative areas of composition, Lucy Hopper, (age 14)

Oil pastel of guitar and bottle, Jon Ake (age 14)

Ten-minute sketch of guitar in line and wash, Shannon Jacobs (age 14)

Sketches from out-of-doors subjects such as this motorcycle provide practice in capturing fleeting light effects, and they can be finished later in the classroom

Oil pastel of bike, Lindon Schultz, (age 12)

Chalk drawing developing abstractions from motorcycle, Louise Robeck (age 14)

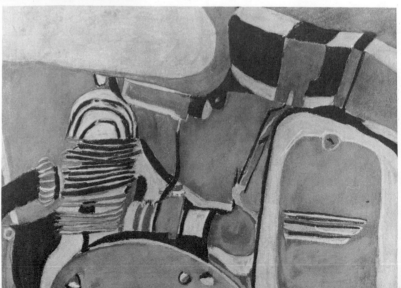

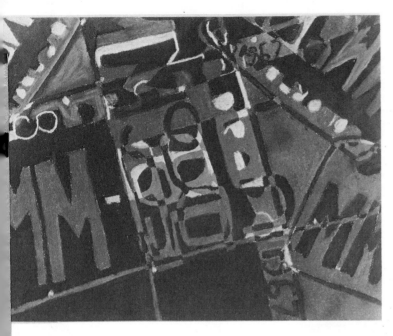

Chalk drawing of abstraction from license plate, Debra Tow, (age 14)

Pencil (2B) drawing using light and dark values to achieve optical effects, Steve Pumphery (age 14)

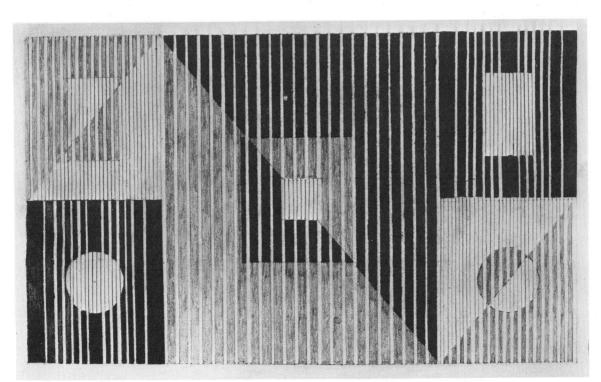

Shapes and surface decoration on this 1951
MG sportscar make it a fascinating drawing
subject. (Photo by Phillips)

Continuous line contour pencil drawing of the
MG, Steve Sandford (age 12)

Thirty-minute contour sketch completed during a trip to the school parking lot, Greg Hansen (age 13)

Pen-and-ink design, emphasizing a variety of line and composition approaches, Tony Till-quist (age 14)

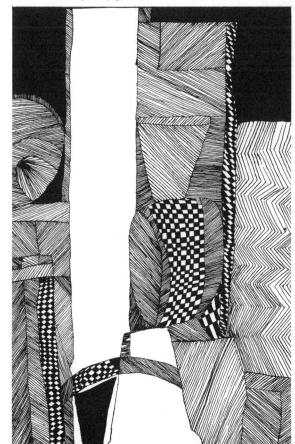

Pen-and-ink abstraction from wheel and headlight form, John Freeze (age 13)

Transfer drawing, Lynette Whiteburch (age 14)

Interpretive drawing, mixed media, Jimmy Parker (age 14)

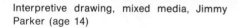

Oil pastel with emphasis on smudging techniques, Kim Stieghorst (age 14)

studio painting

Watercolor wash, wet-in-wet technique,
Donna Gibson (age 13)

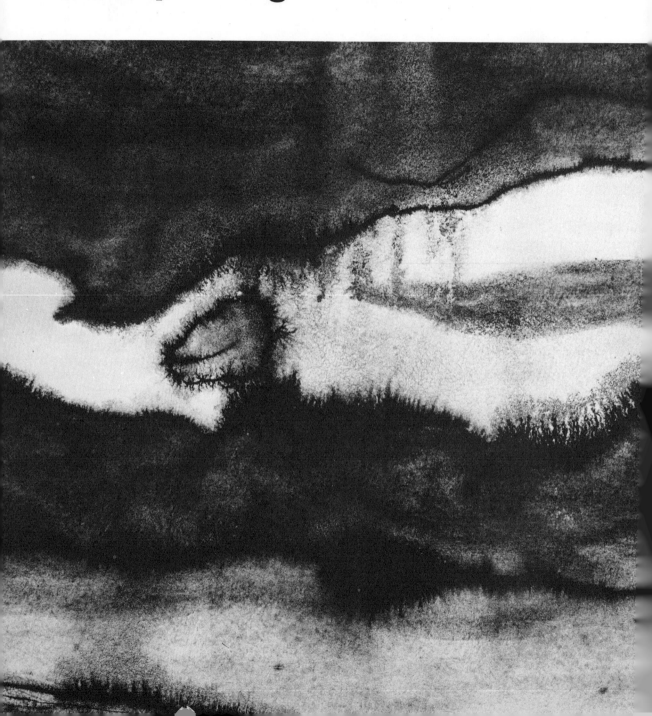

Painting is a two-dimensional art that amplifies the skill of the draftsman. From line, composition, and shading, studied in the drawing unit, a new world of color, texture, and transparency opens up.

A studio that has served well for drawing is adaptable to a painting unit without much rearrangement of furniture. Although art-class painting is generally done on tables, drawing boards come in handy for taping down finished paintings so that a young artist can stand back and observe his work critically. Easels are not often available for all students but if the artist-teacher has strong painting skills of his own he should by all means bring in his easel and set it in a corner of the room for demonstrations and exhibition of his work. And, if the class is not large, perhaps all of the students can work at the easel before the unit is over.

In most communities there are good painters who would be happy to demonstrate watercolor or acrylics for the class. It is essential for students to see how artists physically execute a painting. As useful as they may be in developing skills, table-top exercises alone may leave students with the notion that all "real" artists wear berets and smocks and stand at an easel with a sparklingly clean hand palette.

Still lifes and models should be used extensively in painting as well as drawing, and some of the necessary materials may be on hand already. Before starting, however, the class needs a chance to prepare itself for the added ranges of color and texture they will be asked to respond to. The resource center is very important in this visual preparation. Examples of fine painting techniques can be found in the magazines and books there, and its audio-visual equipment is necessary for showing slides and films.

Any art teacher who has taught beginning students knows that if he asks them to paint what they see around them every day he will get far too many pictures of boxlike houses, stick-shaped apple trees, and cotton-wad clouds with a yellow sun peeping out from behind them. We should never take it for granted that young people can see because, in fact, everyone must be trained for visual awareness. The rust on barrels, textures, colors in the grain of wood, shadows, light on water — all can be brought dramatically into focus in the classroom with a slide projector. Even more effective is the use of slides that the students have taken themselves. In every class there are a few students who own or have access to a 35mm camera, and there is no better assignment for some Saturday than to have them take a series of slides of the buildings, landscapes, people, plants, streams, and any other interesting shape or texture they find within walking distance of the art room.

Some good short 16mm films are easily available for showing in the classroom. In addition to those on painters themselves (*Yankee Painter*, on Winslow Homer's life and art, is an excellent one), there are beautiful films that are works of two-dimensional art in themselves: *The Red Balloon, Dream of Wild Horses, Man — A Course of Study**. Showing films such as these is a sure-fire way to raise interest in the students and at the same time start them on a habit of really looking at their surroundings. This visual preparation unit should be no less than a week.

In keeping with the studio-art approach, the best painting materials available should be used rather than cheaper, poor-quality general issues. Although the cost of expendable materials in the classroom has undoubtedly risen with the years, we found that it averaged less than three cents a day per student — not a very high figure in any case. This reasonable budget would allow for good student-quality brushes, papers, and paints. Oils are too expensive (and too hard to store while in use) for most schools.

The greatest handicap to painting in public school is probably the lack of good brushes. There should be at least three nylon brushes (numbers 6, 8, and 12) and two squirrel brushes (numbers 6 and 8) for each student in the class. Such brushes last much longer than those of poor quality, and are therefore well worth the investment. Most stores will offer teachers samples if a large order is anticipated, and it is wise to sample and test the wide variety of brushes on the market before purchasing. Students can usually find 2-inch or 3-inch flat brushes and interesting odd brushes at home to keep in their painting kits.

Painting paper should be good quality too. Watercolor paper should be at least 70-pound press. Tempera and acrylics can be used on white detail drawing paper, heavy construction paper, and heavy manila paper.

After the visual preparation unit, a series of painting units in different media can be undertaken, each lasting a few weeks. At the beginning of a unit the class should spend three or four days in simple brush exercises, including dry-brush and graded washes done on newsprint and either thrown away or used for quick critiques later on, as the students benefit from comparing their new skills with their own first attempts and with other students' work. During a unit, students should work from the figure, still lifes, and sketches made outside the classroom — all skills that have been previously introduced in the drawing unit. As in drawing, composition should be emphasized, and with each new exercise, a fast, light sketch should be made before any painting begins.

---

*The films may be obtained at the following distributors: *Yankee Painter* — Contemporary Films, 330 W. 42 St., New York, N.Y. 10036; *The Red Balloon* — Brandon Films, Inc., 221 W. 57 St., New York, N.Y. 10019; *Man — A Course of Study* — Modern Learning Aids, P.O. Box 302, Rochester, N.Y. 14603.

No one can say exactly how long an individual group of students needs to spend in each activity before moving on. Certainly, some degree of skill must be attained, but intellectual comprehension is equally important. What is the student trying to express? How is he trying to make others see it and feel it? Each student should be able to answer these questions through critiques and by constant reference to slides and prints in the resource center. Following each unit the class should easily be able to identify that particular medium or technique in reproductions of paintings. But don't let them copy — copying another painting offers far too much of a crutch, while learning through exposure to different styles helps to prepare students for in-depth work in future classes.

The first specific watercolor problem might be a still life from live potted plants or paper flowers. In two or three class periods there is an opportunity to learn wash techniques and develop an ability to manipulate the intricacies of transparency and composition.

The second problem might be a still life from an arrangement of fruits and vegetables, with one period devoted to wet-in-wet technique, one to dry-brush, and one to wet-in-dry. After studying the realistic aspects of their compositions, the students might be interested in trying an abstract, in the manner of Klee, Marin, or Picasso.

Basic watercolor techniques will have prepared the students for quick, fresh studies from the figure or a complex form such as a motorcycle. The unit might end with a free choice of interpretive study based on sketches made outside the class.

A concentrated tempera unit should encompass no less than two weeks. The freshness and brilliance of tempera offer an opportunity to teach control of color combinations, textures, and values. Although a number of problems can be developed from setups similar to those used in watercolor, at least a few should be based on nearby landscape studies. Landscape, in its broadest meaning, is the physical aspect of the community in which we live, and students will discover a new view of their world as they search for subjects to paint.

Acrylics, offering qualities of both transparent watercolors and tempera, give students a chance to experiment with skill areas in which they were not originally successful. This medium encourages students to work fast, since it dries so quickly, and therefore is appropriate at the end of the painting sequence. Acrylics retain their transparency without blending them as watercolors do, thus preventing the muddy tones that so often occur in student watercolors. As the last unit, work in acrylics should be flexible enough to vary with student interest and the length of time allotted for painting in the course.

Few students without training can distinguish between museum-quality painting, genuine folk art, and mass-produced paintings from the discount store. Throughout the painting unit, there should be an emphasis on the essential difference between good and poor painting. Students these days grow up in a world of discount-store art — bullfighters on black velvet, Spanish galleons, and little dogs and children with big sad eyes. Most art students will not become artists; they will, however, all be consumers. The artist-teacher, therefore, has a responsibility beyond the teaching of techniques. He must help his students to become culturally aware enough to make wise choices and astute judgments about painting.

Loose contour pencil drawing (6B) washed over, Susan Williams (age 13)

Even a modest budget allows for good-quality brushes and paper — and that often makes a big difference in the quality of the work. (Photo by Unity)

Painting is an outgrowth of the interpretive line and wash techniques learned in the drawing unit. Wash line design, Keith Parker (age 14)

During each medium unit, students should work from still lifes, figures, and outdoor sketches — all previously practiced skills. Watercolor, transparent techniques, Martin Buick (age 13)

Tempera contour drawing, Mark Burrow (age 14)

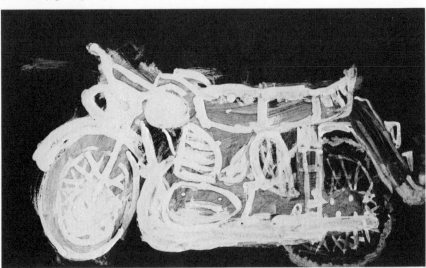

Girl with Violet Face, oil pastel from the figure, Mark Thompson (age 14)

Girl and Doll, oil pastel from the figure, Sue Miller (age 14)

White-line tempera painting into wash on dark paper, Kenny Earl (age 14)

Three Heads, acrylic, felt-tip pen, and mixed media, Danny Persichehi (age 13)

Four Heads, oil pastel, contour-line drawing, Melanie Hill (age 13)

Girl, mixed-media collage, Debby Powell (age 15)

Aztec Woman, oil pastel, Alex Bugel (age 13)

Head of Boy, acrylic from the figure, Robert Tenny (age 14)

Auto Parts, tempera, Kurt Samuelson (age 14)

Red Baron, acrylic, Gregg Seastone (age 14)

Figures, tissue paper and felt-tip pen, Dan Byrnes (age 13)

Phone, tempera from a still life, Cathy Connor
(age 13)

Girl with Black Face, oil pastel from the figure,
Tim Sewolt (age 13)

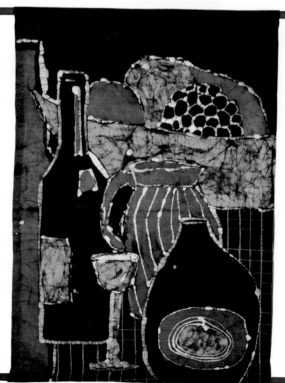

Green Wine Bottle, batik, Debbie Theander
(age 14)

Chair-Wall Design, mixed-media collage, Don Taylor (age 14)

Circle Form, woven construction done without
a loom, Cindy Penn (age 14)

Tempera, Kim Taylor (age 13)

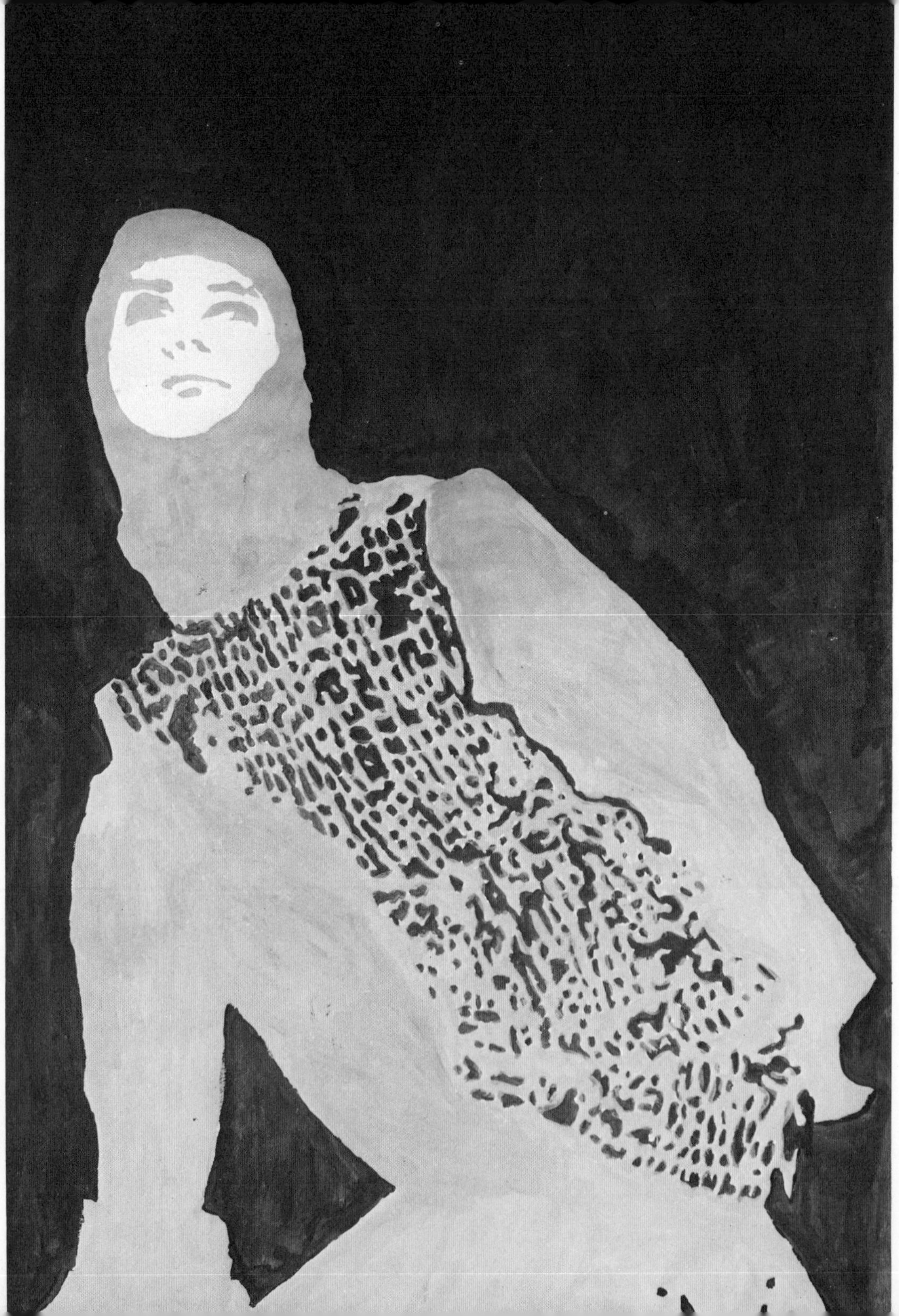

Acrylic, from the figure, Claudette Thomas (age 14). Emphasis is on opaque techniques and brush styles

studio printmaking

Hockey Player, woodcut, Brian Clark, (age 13). Composition is developed by carving away the foreground into completely negative space

Printmaking includes such a vast range of skills and different techniques that it hardly can be more than introduced in a general art program. It is just this wide range that gives the unit its excitement — the artist-teacher must concentrate on areas he is familiar with and interested in himself, and the class and teacher together can experiment with new materials and methods.

Needless to say, printmaking depends directly on the previous drawing and painting units. Cutting, etching, inking, or dyeing must follow the same line, composition, and shading principles as sketching does; all that has been learned about colors in the painting unit must now be carefully preplanned to transfer it to the indirect processes of printmaking. If experiments in contrasting papers and pigments have been done, such as those shown on page . . . . ., the principles of relief line that printmakers use will be that much easier for students to grasp.

The indirect nature of printmaking requires first of all more equipment and secondly more forethought than the direct two-dimensional arts. This refinement can be an advantage if it teaches students to plan more carefully, just as some limitation of school equipment can sometimes make a teacher more inventive with the printmaking materials he has.

Units in printmaking can vary from four to nine weeks, or even extend for a full year, depending on what the teacher is interested in and what facilities can be built into the budget. Some of our programs included sophisticated methods like silk-screening and etching from traditional copper plates or contemporary plastic ones. In this chapter, only basic methods, linoleum-block printing and woodblock printing, are discussed. Supplies are not expensive, and the procedures can be carried out in any studio-art classroom. Cutting, inking, and printing can be done at a student's own desk or work space, although precautions should be taken that the students are not crowded when they are using cutting tools. A clothesline hung from one end of the room to the other is a very useful innovation for drying prints attached to it by ordinary clothespins. Ink, which has to be rolled out before it can be transferred to a block, can be worked on large sheets of glass set up on a conveniently located stand or even rolled right on the formica surface that is used on most art-room tables.

Many schools are willing to buy large pieces of equipment such as those used in industrial-arts shops, but budgets need not be excessive for printmaking. It is not necessary to have a press, although it can be an exciting introduction to the technology of printmaking. All the prints shown here were made with spoon-burnishing and water-based inks.

Only one-third of the schools in our program had presses; some were ordering them and some were spending the money on needs they felt were more important. A good press costs between $600 and $1800. Inexpensive presses, advertised in most catalogs, are really toys — they have a small bed and do not hold up well under constant use. It is better to wait until the purchase of a good press can be justified than to get a cheap one that will soon have to be replaced.

Materials are not expensive either. Linoleum — of the gray "battleship linoleum" variety — can be purchased in large uncut rolls from stores that sell linoleum tile. This particular kind is more pliable than other linoleums, which chip and tear easily. Buying in rolls saves approximately 75 per cent of the cost of blocks premounted on plywood, and the rolls can be cut and mounted later with the aid of school shop equipment or by the students themselves, as part of the unit. White pine for woodblocks is inexpensive, readily available in all areas, and easily laminated to form a block (here the shop's vises will come in handy). Wood should be free of knots and relatively soft. If students are purchasing supplies, they should be warned that plywood and other hard woods are difficult to cut.

There are many inexpensive wood-cutting and linoleum-cutting tools on the market but they too should be avoided because they do not stay sharp and thus are a waste of time as well as a hazard. Struggling with dull tools causes more accidents than cutting with sharp ones. It is better to buy good, durable tools and good sharpening stones than poor-quality, inexpensive ones.

Paper and ink should not be difficult or costly to obtain either. Linoleum blocks work well with water-based ink, and proofs can be taken on newspaper or newsprint. Woodblocks print better with oil-based ink, which is more expensive, but if the printmaking unit includes silkscreening or other techniques that call for such ink, the cost can be spread out. As for papers, newsprint and tissue (both colored and white) are inexpensive while charcoal paper and printmaking paper in a variety of weights and textures are more suitable for advanced classes. There is no limit to the variety of papers, textures, and colors that can be used. Brayers come in different materials and hardnesses; before deciding what to buy, the artist-teacher should consider the needs of all the different kinds of printmaking that will be covered.

Most students have even less experience with printmaking than they do with drawing and painting, and demonstrations are very important. These can be live or on film, as in the particularly fine *Eskimo Artist Kenojuak**, which records the efforts of a young Eskimo mother as she attempts to interpret her feelings about her environment. Students should have a chance to see plates, screens, and blocks as well as finished prints.

*This film can be obtained at Contemporary Films, 330 W. 42 St., New York, N.Y. 10036

There is no magic like the magic of pulling a print. When a new visual image appears on paper after a student has cut it into wood or linoleum, he suddenly becomes aware of the transforming power of surface texture. Texture is the key to the printmaking unit. A few days should be spent concentrating on simple direct rubbings from classroom surfaces — wood, metal, cloth, foil. Three days or four days of homework at the same time can cover rubbings from decorative surfaces on municipal buildings, churches, schools, gravestones, manhole covers, and furniture. Since the surfaces inside the classroom are generally less interesting than those outside, it is a good idea to discuss and display these homework rubbings in class as part of the visual orientation to texture.

A good first step in the printmaking unit is a demonstration of safe, effective cutting techniques. Students must be taught to draw knives and gouges away from themselves, rather than toward their bodies, and sharpening procedures can be introduced at this point to stress the fact that sharp tools cause fewer accidents than dull ones. The different textures created by different blades should be demonstrated, too.

Results will be more artistically satisfying — and students will take the unit more seriously — if work is done on large blocks right from the beginning. No print should be less than 12 x 12 inches, and larger if possible. If allowed to work directly on the surface without preplanning, many students take refuge in some trite image they have already practiced drawing — a "Snoopy" dog or a peace symbol, perhaps. However, after having completed the drawing and painting sequences of the course, they are well able to sketch out their ideas. Several sketches should be made before a strong design is chosen and transferred to the surface of the block.

Since water-based ink is easier to work with, it is a good idea to use linoleum before wood. Although several days will be spent in transferring and cutting the design, inking and printing are relatively quick procedures. If water-based ink is used for the first prints, it is even possible to print more than one color in a single period. The first color can be drying while the block is washed off and reinked. For two- or three-color prints, a demonstration is necessary to teach the class about register.

A second unit of several weeks can be for woodblock printing. If the blocks are not ready-made, the students might begin by laminating them to the proper thickness and sanding the surface with equipment borrowed from the school shop. Or, if scheduling permits, the whole art class can work in the shop. Oil-based inks work better on a woodblock, and several prints can be taken from a block inked this way. After this small edition is completed, the students can number them properly, and learn about printmaker's editions from looking at prints in the resource center.

Most printmaking experiences in school art are limited to a small linoleum-block cut that is completed — from design to print — in approximately three days. In studio-art printmaking, the teacher should extend the unit's meaning and continuity further than this — by working with large blocks, by having students draw several designs for the blocks, and by using the blocks as a lead-in to the three-dimensional unit that follows. The three-dimensional cut blocks can be used as an assemblage on an art-room door, as a room divider, or as interesting art forms hung on the wall.

There are unlimited options in printmaking. Once students discover simple printmaking techniques, they can incorporate them into woodcuts, linoleum blocks, cardboard prints, collagraphs, and many other methods. An experimental area set aside during this unit quite often rewards both class and teacher. Students can try rolling brayers over wire, feathers, or other surfaces, and then inking the block — or painting directly with the roller on paper. They can distress the surface of the woodblock by pounding it with wire and other objects, and experiment with the vast number of variables in multicolor printing. While the brayers are still wet, they can wrap them with yarn, roll them in ink, and ink the surface of the block. Then after unwrapping, the brayers are cleaned on scraps of cardboard, and the cardboard surfaces are also printed. The more experimentation the class does, the more aware they become of how many printmaking possibilities are waiting to be explored.

At the beginning of the unit a demonstration in proper cutting techniques — for safety and variation of line — should be given. Nuns, linoleum-block print with varied cutting techniques, Sara King (age 15)

Linoleum-block print, Ann Shaw, (age 15)

Several sketches should be made before a design is chosen and the cutting begins. Linoleum block print, abstraction from motorcycle, Diane Armenta, (age 15)

Woodcut, Janice Jenkins (age 14). Emphasis is on light and dark pattern

Woodcut, Bobbie Slight (age 14). Emphasis is on positive and negative space in composition

The indirect nature of printmaking helps students refine their compositions. Linoleum block print from photograph of astronaut, Kevin Bowles (age 13). The source has been stylized to achieve light and dark patterns

Woodcut, Steve White (age 14)

Texture is the key to a printmaking unit — here wood grain emphasizes emotion. Wood-cut, Cheryl Mortenson (age 14)

Jenny, woodcut, Kathy States (age 12)

Woodcut with background texture achieved by pounding wire into surface of wood, Patty Norris (age 14)

Woodcut with tool marks made in the surface of the wood, Faith Jordan (age 14)

Woodcut, Karen Williams (age 14) (Photo by Unity)

Woodcut, Becky Angus,
(age 14)

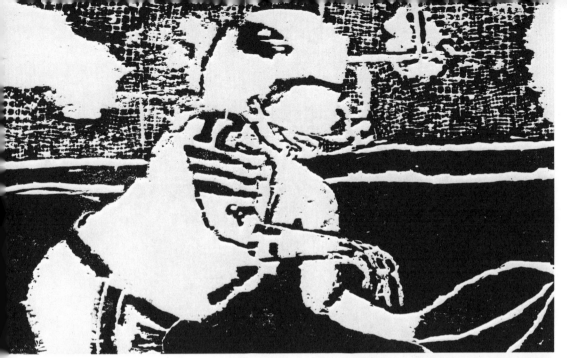

Quarterback, woodcut, Dave Harmon, (age 12)

Woodcut, Daryl Cook (age 13). The surface was distressed by pounding wire and bolts into the wood

Woodcut, John Mangusso (age 13)

Two Moons, cardboard print, Eric Luck (age 14). Different layers of a cardboard sheet were cut away and then overprinted

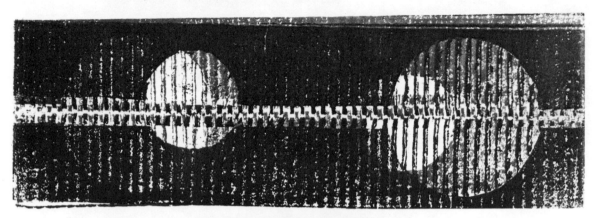

Printmaking has almost unlimited variations, which can be explored as time and talent permit. Two-color woodcut, Doug Cherry (age 14)

Woodcut, Scott Richardson (age 14)

studio three-dimensional design

Students can learn the principles of aesthetic form through a program in artistic crafts. Fine ceramics, artist-teacher Ken Aden's work, are displayed in the classroom.

Three-dimensional design is often taught through the medium of sculpture. In a public-school art program, however, the length of time and amount of materials needed to complete a sculpture and the technical facilities needed to carve or cast it are prohibitive. We have found that an alternate way to introduce students into the study of design, unity, and aesthetic form is through a program of artistic crafts. Sculpture can be done in any medium — clay, textiles, wood, plastics.

Studio three-dimensional design is not the usual crafts program, although it has the strong appeal of allowing the student to "do something with his hands." Students should understand from the start, however, that the crafts kits and how-to-do-it catalogs with which they are already familiar are really examples of how *not* to do it. Crafts is one of the weakest areas of most art-school programs because not enough time is spent in this kind of orientation to design.

Students can sometimes more easily identify good design in objects that they do not think of as "artistic." The teacher should try to bring in or show slides of industrial objects that are well designed, of jewelry, of functional pottery and china, of finely woven blankets and clothing. The contrast of these utilitarian objects with examples of fine-art sculpture, enameling, artistic ceramics, and art fabrics can then be more pointedly made. Visual orientation to design in crafts is important because so many students think of crafts as something mass-produced and sold in curio shops or done in summer camps on rainy days. Crafts can be a serious medium of artistic expression, as a visit to a craftsman's studio will show. If this cannot be arranged there are some good films to help motivate the class, such as *Potters of the USA,* or ABC television's film *With These Hands**.

Several of our schools are now offering ceramics and crafts on a semester basis, and it is not uncommon to have one-quarter of the student body request such a course. We are discovering that student demand for courses that will allow working with the hands in an artistic way is continually increasing and that these skills are merely challenged rather than satisfied by once-over-quickly courses, even at the elementary-school level. Some schools, anticipating this demand, have divided their art programs. One teacher concentrates on two-dimensional design and the other on three-dimensional design. An arrangement like this allows for total planning of two separate art rooms around their special needs, and gives much flexibility in room utilization and curriculum organization.

*These films can be obtained at the following distributors: *Potters of the U.S.A.* — McGraw-Hill Films, 330 W. 42 St., New York, N.Y.; *With These Hands* — Daniel Wilson Productions, Inc., 267 W. 25 St., New York, N.Y. 10001.

If, as is more likely the case, a single teacher must take responsibility for drawing, painting, and printmaking as well as three-dimensional design, by the time he gets to the crafts unit he may feel he is juggling skills and techniques in a three-ring circus. The teacher who tries to offer more than a few choices of craft activities at one time invariably finds that he cannot provide proper demonstrations or enough individualized instruction to keep the class actively involved. Crafts activities are somewhat more individualized than group drawing, for example, but with proper concentration on a few activities each student will be able to do meaningful work. The illustrations in this chapter were taken from programs with full classes in which the artist-teacher either concentrated on one craft at a time or allowed several to go on at once — not more than four though — after thorough preparation for each.

To help prevent confusion, a room that has been used as a studio for two-dimensional art should be totally rearranged and cleared of anything that can get dirty. New space arrangements are needed for setting up potter's wheels, for wedging and building clay areas, for tables and workbenches to spread out large expanses of cloth, for free areas for frames, looms, dye baths, wood-sawing, and assorted activities. Even storage rooms way down at the end of the hall may have to be pressed into service for the bulky projects that will be forthcoming. Perhaps a separate section of the room can be set aside for preparation and clean-up, which take more time in this unit than others, and better students might be appointed as "lab assistants" to help before and after the class is at work. Half the class may end up sitting around without materials or ideas unless some steps are taken to see that all the students have a clear understanding of the materials and preparations they need for their projects.

At too many schools the whole subject of crafts is covered in the period of a week — the student is given a pound or two of clay and the opportunity to make an ashtray. Why not plan this adaptable unit jointly with the students? The particular crafts areas chosen should be a compromise between what the students are most interested in and what the teacher is best able to demonstrate. A local craftsman, or even an upper-classman who is skilled in a particular craft, might be willing to demonstrate in additional areas.

The problem of budget is both more and less difficult to handle in this unit than in the others. Programs can easily be adapted to available materials, yet there is expensive equipment that can make crafts easier and more exciting: potter's wheels, electric or gas kilns, looms and frames. Instead of purchasing inexpensive pieces that may cause more trouble than they are worth, the teacher should budget for one area at a time and use hand techniques in the others. Then, as the school's collection of tools and equipment grows, the course can gradually be expanded into more mechanized techniques. If there is no money for buying a loom or a frame for hooking rugs, 1-inch x 2-inch boards and some string can be used for good functional substitutes. If there are no wheels, the majority of time can be spent in hand-built constructions.

Most school ceramics programs are equipped with an electric kiln. While adequate, these do not allow for reduction firing, cannot handle as large a load in the firing chamber, and are costly to maintain. Consideration should be given to building a gas kin — they are much less complicated than many people believe. The ceramics shown in this book were fired in gas kilns.

Ceramics is usually the first craft exploration undertaken. During the unit, the studio should look like a potters' workshop if possible — beg or borrow good clay pots from local sources to display in the room. If no beautiful pots can be found, perhaps a trip to the museum may unearth some interesting examples. Far too few students are aware of the range of pottery and of the exciting shapes and textures that can be made so easily in this plastic medium, and then permanently held by firing.

To begin a clay unit, the students should do a series of texture problems and build simple coil, slab, and pinch pots using principles of design he has learned. It is better *not* to save the work done at this stage, just as first sketches and line exercises were not saved, so that the student sees his work as part of a learning experience, and feels free to experiment. From these basic exercises, more interpretively sculptural forms can be created, with or without the aid of a potter's wheel. The use of glazes and other surface-enrichment techniques stresses the continuity of ceramics with other units in the program.

Part of a textile project could be research into the many supply and information sources that have recently become available with the growing popularity of the textile crafts. Exciting materials are inexpensive and easy to find, and provide unlimited resources for new ideas. Contemporary macrame, hooking, weaving, and stitchery are often abstract rather than functional in concept, and therefore a unit in the textile arts requires heavy emphasis on the teaching of design. Much preplanning in the form of sketches and student-teacher conferences should be done before the student begins his project.

Two-dimensional arts have been taught for so long in traditional art programs that to many art teachers they seem to teach themselves in an obvious, logical sequence of skills. Crafts rely more on the creative resources of the individual teacher, and the the unit may seem to take more organization and planning (and the preparation and clean-up may take more patience) than drawing, painting, and printmaking. Yet, for all the difficulties, this unit has a chance of reaching those students who did not succeed in earlier units. Each time a young person finds an opportunity to express himself in a new medium, he is making art that much more important in his life.

New space arrangements are needed for setting up potter's wheels and other crafts equipment

An interesting functional form can be contrasted with fine-art sculpture

Ringo, wood construction, soft white pine and tempera. This six-foot sculpture was an eighth-grade class project

Slab pottery by eighth-grade students. Many satisfying ceramic forms can be created without a potter's wheel — hand-built coil, slab, and pinch pots. (Photo by Phillips)

A texture problem in abstract forms and surfaces is developed from modeling paste and cheesecloth, Howard Crouch (age 15)

Hand-built pots with decorative designs and cloth textures by eighth-grade students

Ceramic bottles by eighth-grade students.
The teacher reviewed pre-Columbian ceramic
art forms before the class began work

Beginning hand-built pottery, 8 to 14 inches
high, by eighth-grade students

Modeled from clay, fixed, and painted with acrylics, these ceramic food sculptures were an eighth-grade class project that introduced some of the ideas of Pop Art. (Photo by Phillips)

Surface design: hooked rug and hand-built coil pots (by ninth-grade students) benefit from the knowledge gained in drawing, painting, and printmaking units

Contemporary textile arts are often abstract rather than functional, and the unit requires teaching of design principles

Hooked rugs and frames by ninth-grade students

conclusion

I am thoroughly convinced that art is the most exciting part of a school's curriculum. The atmosphere of an art-studio classroom can reflect that excitement, that magic. It can and should be a gallery, a resource area, a studio, a visually exciting stimulus for learning. By its appearance alone it becomes a stage for the curriculum that is designed around it.

Television, movies, and travel have given us a new kind of student. He needs the knowledge that art has to offer so that he can sift through the bombardment of visual information that he receives. Students who leave the studio should be prepared not only to draw and paint but to recognize good and bad architecture, to be sensitive to the need for environmental planning — in other words, they should become visually aware.

If we are to justify art education, it must become more than what it has been in the past. Students have passed through our classes without ever having been exposed to taste, judgment, or awareness. For proof of this, we need only look at our ugly environment of billboards and flashing signs, at the tawdry art and architecture that people buy and support. Art can and should be an essential course in our schools. It must be relevant to the world the students live in, and most important, it should leave them with a commitment to improve the aesthetic quality of the environment that they will leave for their children. No greater challenge faces any educator in America today.